T0078392

SIGNIFICANT TO

GOD

You Matter to Him

JOANN JORDAN

WESTBOW
PRESS®
A DIVISION OF THOMAS NELSON
& ZONDERVAN

WestBow Press books may be ordered through booksellers or by contacting:

WestBow Press
A Division of Thomas Nelson & Zondervan
1663 Liberty Drive
Bloomington, IN 47403
www.westbowpress.com
844-714-3454

Scriptures taken from the Holy Bible, New International Version®, NIV®.
Copyright © 1973, 1978, 1984, 2011 by Biblica, Inc.™ Used by permission
of Zondervan. All rights reserved worldwide. www.zondervan.com The
"NIV" and "New International Version" are trademarks registered in
the United States Patent and Trademark Office by Biblica, Inc.®

ISBN: 978-1-6642-1203-9 (sc)
ISBN: 978-1-6642-1202-2 (e)

Library of Congress Control Number: 2020922242

Print information available on the last page.

WestBow Press rev. date: 12/09/2020

CONTENTS

INTRODUCTION

This book introduces five familiar Bible stories. These stories are about truth with imagination. The five short stories are about children without naming them.

As you are introduced to each one, may you understand that they were children who were quite normal. As each child's story is read, keep in mind that these could be children you may know. Also they too can have an amazing story.

Children need to know that God sees them differently than folks they may encounter daily. God sees the possibilities they can become. He loves each one individually, just as He did the children who made the best-selling book ever.

When a child feels left out, bullied, unnoticed, or neglected, God keeps a record. He knows your heart, your situation, and your name.

God has passion for those who seem to always be the last one chosen or invited or ignored by their peers. You can rest assured that God has you and He loves you. The Father knows the longing of your heart and wants you to succeed in life by being happy. Know you have a heavenly Father who takes you to places in life where He can love you the most. He will lead you if you trust Him, as the children did in these five short stories.

Trust in the God of the heavens. He created you for His good pleasure, and He desires to share eternity with you. Come along and let's travel back three thousand years ago to watch how God was real in every story, just as He is in the story of the reader today. *Significant to God* are short stories to illustrate how you matter to Him!

THE LAD

JOHN 6

Early mornings bring a smile as she prepares to bake bread for the day and the Sabbath tomorrow. Gazing for a moment out her window, her eyes catch the flash of a peeking sun rising over the cliffs. Glancing quickly, she continues to work, but a tune that escapes her lips enhances her smile.

Six or more? Perhaps twelve, she thinks. She rolls the dough and then turns it ever so slightly to give it a fullness it needs. She places it on the fire to cook. Barley has a better price than wheat. Though coarse, it has a flavor she likes. Taste is important to her.

Arrangements were made last evening for their son to have a free day to roam and hike across the cliffs. He is like a young gazelle. He is a good son and smart. His schooling will start soon, and he will be instructed in a craft and the ways of men. He will be entering bar mitzvah. He will know his responsibilities as an adult. His dad will instruct him on what he should know of the scriptures. He will recite at temple his knowledge and responsibilities.

With the bread now baking, she cooks the rest of the meal for the men who are preparing to start their day. Her husband is going with the village men. They fish daily, except for the Sabbath. Fish and bread are their daily nourishment. Still humming, she finishes the rest of the table, serving the eggs and bread as the men enter the room.

She is blessed and content in her home. Some of the village

ladies are mistreated, and their husbands are drinkers. They consume too much and create disgraceful problems. Her heart is grateful. Her husband says the prayer as they start the meal, and she smiles. She has all she needs right here in this room. The morning is quiet, and the woman and her husband are thinking about their day.

She is busily packing her son's knapsack, wondering if she should pack three or two breads and three or two fishes. She decides on three loaves and two fish, ties the knapsack together, and sets it aside. During quiet time for her today, she will weave for a while and start the making of clothing for winter. It has been on her mind. Knowing the sheep are sheared, she has enough wool to prepare two coats and warm clothing for the cold that will come quickly. She enjoys the quiet. It is a reflective time for her.

Breakfast is finished, and after clearing the table and preparing to weave, her son comes and gets his bag. He smiles and tells her goodbye. Now her husband goes, saying he will see her before sunset. She is alone and happy.

Across the cliffs, goats roam, and so does the boy. It's his favorite time. He has freedom from schooling. Knowing his birthday is soon, he yearns to hike the cliff and wander for a while. His mind is thinking of the future, which it seems has caught up with him. Thirteen is the age of accountability, and his father has been talking with him about responsibilities and his craft. Today, he will pray and reflect on where he is headed.

Coming over the highest cliff, he can see the Sea of Galilee. From his peak, the blue waters are beautiful. He stands there thinking. He wants to get over the cliff and eat his food by the water, which is always his favorite place.

His heart is happy. He watches the gazelles playing on the cliff in front of him. It is a wonder to watch how they glide, skip, and jump over the cliff, as if it is not difficult and dangerous. They cause him to laugh aloud. How silly they are pushing each other off the side and then waiting to see if they get tagged back. The wonder of nature and the creatures made by Jehovah is such a beauty.

Suddenly a movement catches his attention. His eyes slightly squint. He tries to see what is happening far down off the cliffs. He has climbed up very high. It is so hard to see that far, but something is going on. Taking a moment to decide how he will go down, he starts his descent.

The sun is hot today, but high up where he is, it seems cooler. While trying to trek down to the water, he thinks, *Maybe I should have started sooner.* But daydreaming got his timing off.

Now getting closer, he slows down and is stunned to see people everywhere. Men, children, and women are streaming on the shores. There are thousands, multitudes of people. What is happening? He is high enough to get a panoramic view, and it seems that a man has their attention. He decides he will stay high enough and go toward the man, who is walking ahead of the people.

As he approaches across the cliff, from his viewpoint it seems a group of men are guarding this one person. Listening intently, the boy can hear him speaking. His voice echoes across the cliffs and the water, and he has sat down right now. So as the lad watches and listens from a distance, he can tell the speaker is a man of authority. He speaks clearly and distinctly. He can be heard from far away. The crowd is large, but it is quiet, as if a person of great stature were in their midst, and they are reverent of him.

Almost reaching the same area, the boy too becomes quiet and listens intently as the man speaks. Now he sits down, higher than the people, but in a perfect position to hear the words and yet go higher to get away if need be.

This man named Jesus speaks to the people like a gentle father to a child. He is explaining to them about the blessings that will be theirs when they are obedient to the law. He tells them to be salt and light and then says heaven will be their reward.

By now, it is afternoon, and the lad has heard the man speak. He is so interested that he has forgotten his lunch. Just as he thinks about his stomach, a man comes up behind him and asks what his lunch is. Startled, he looks at this stranger and asks who he is.

The man replies, "Andrew. The Master has need of your lunch."

Quickly, he hands Andrew his lunch and follows him down to the man, whom he called Master.

As he watches, the Master takes the bread and fish and blesses them, and then they begin to multiply right from his hands. The men, who seem to be his group, begin serving fish and loaves across the sea of people who had been advised to sit down in groups. Quickly, each man comes to the Master, and with a basket each filled, they go out and return for more until every man, woman, and child has been fed. The Master looks at the lad, and in turn, the boy is speechless. He is overwhelmed by what he has witnessed and knows in his spirit that this is no ordinary man.

As the men gather up the overflow, they bring it to the Master. He motions to the lad, but the boy is so dumbfounded that he shakes his head and cannot receive any leftovers. It is as if there were a bell. The Master rises and heads away from everyone, and the crowd is advised to go home, as the next day is the Sabbath.

The lad is also left pondering all he has witnessed, and going over a different route, he too goes home. Tomorrow he will look for this man when they go to the temple for prayer.

As he approaches his home, he can see his mother putting candles on the tables and his dad just washing his hands. They both look up as he enters the room. Does he look different? He sure feels different. Will he be able to explain what happened today? Will they believe him? He can hardly believe what he witnessed.

Quickly washing his hands and feet, he prepares for the evening meal. The day is closing as the sun goes down behind the mountains. As they are waiting, his mother says the prayer.

As the morning sun comes up, the mother is busily preparing the food for the Sabbath. It is an early day for the family, as they will walk to Capernaum to make a sacrifice for their son's birthday. She is full of joy that he will now be recognized as a man by the village and at the temple. It is her first time to be able to hear him speak to the elders. His father and the rabbi have prepared him for this day.

Dressing quickly in his clothes, never worn before and sewn with loving hands, he places his shawl around his shoulders. He's excited to be going to temple but even more hopeful at seeing the man, Jesus. He is sure he will see him, as he had heard the men— Andrew and others—mention Jesus could be attending. The boy wants his parents to meet Jesus even more so than he wants them to see his part at the meeting. It is hard for the lad to try to keep to himself what he witnessed yesterday, but self-control is important, and learning to wait is good sense.

Both Father and Mother are ready, and they begin the journey down the road with friends and family who are supporting his time of age. But they too will sacrifice. It is an important time on the Sabbath.

Entering Capernaum, crowds become dense, and a lot of people are going toward the temple. As they walk, the lad begins looking everywhere for this Jesus. By now they are almost to the temple when he sees a crowd gathering and looking closely. There stands Jesus. The lad yells out with glee, as you do when you see a friend.

The mother turns and glances in the direction he is pointing and sees a crowd surrounding the man as if he were a rabbi. She keeps glancing, trying to figure out what is exciting her son.

Now he speaks. "Father and Mother, come meet my friend Jesus."

Not having hearing that name before, the mother is startled. Her son is speaking of a man the age of her husband. The son pulls his father's arm, and his mother follows. Seeing the man, she smiles as if she does know him.

As they come closer, the rabbi places mud on his hands, puts them over the eyes of old, blind Bartimaeus, and then tells him to wash them clear. As the mother watches, an old woman walking with two sticks speaks to this man, Jesus. He nods and looks up to the sky, and right before her eyes, she sees the old woman drop her sticks and walk as if she were young again. Bartimaeus comes back, kneels at the feet of this man, and thanks him, as he can now see.

Father and Mother are shocked! They have known Bartimaeus for years. He has always been blind, but now he can see. What? Never have they seen such a miracle. The crowd is deep, but the man, the rabbi, sees their son and smiles. The boy stands still, watching as others are healed.

Now the father asks the son, "How do you know him?"

The lad knows now he can tell them what happened yesterday and they will believe. So he tells them the tale of the fish and the loaves. The mother weeps, and the father shakes his head with happiness. He tells them about the five thousand people and how the Master gave them the fish he had caught and the bread his mother had baked to the folks. Humbly they wipe their tears, and Father nods to the Master as they go on to the temple.

It's a glorious day in the life of a thirteen-year-old lad. Yes, it's a glorious day for this family.

 **CHALK TALK**

Meditation
Psalm 1:2; Philippians 4:8; Psalm 19:14

Surrender
Romans 12:2; Isaiah 64:8; Colossians 2:20-23

Respectful
1 Peter 2:17; Hebrews 13:7; Romans 12:10;

Curious
Proverbs 25:2–3; 1 Peter 1:10–11; 1 Corinthians 1:22

Self-control
2 Timothy 1:7; Proverbs 18:21; Titus 1:8

Hardworking
Colossians 3:23; Philippians 2:14–15; Proverbs 12:24

Trustworthy
Colossians 3:9–10; Proverbs 28:26

Listens
James 1:19; 1 John 5:14; Matthew 7:24

Obedient
Proverbs 6:20; Deuteronomy 5:33; Luke 6:27–28; Romans 8:1

 **JOURNAL**

The story tells us about reaching the age of accountability. What do you conclude from the story and scriptures that you may want to apply to your life and share with other friends? Would you be intrigued by the multiplying of food, and would it cause you to want to understand who this man was and how he accomplished this miracle?

Joann Jordan

 JOURNAL

THE PRINCESS

MARK 6:21-29

It was cool and dark inside the palace as she tried to stay close to the stone walls shielded from the sun. It was so hot today. The servants and chambermaids were seeking coolness, and the child was no exception.

They woke her early this morning and bathed her, which she loved, as it helped to cool her down from the dewdrops that had accumulated on her in sleep. Quickly they washed her, massaged her hair, ran cool water to run off all the suds they had used, and prepared her for her bath. Bathing was a ritual she enjoyed twice daily.

Now they combed her hair, shining ebony from the ajowan oils applied to her tanned skin and feet. With skilled hands, they massaged the oils into her childlike body. She squirmed and wiggled, laughing as they tickled her toes. The servants joined in, laughing at this happy, beautiful child.

Perfumed oils gave off a lovely fragrance as she walked the corridors of the king's palace. She liked knowing that the footmen and court ladies were all aware that she was a spoiled and willful child. Impatience was getting to her now, as she was hungry and could smell the foods as they cooked nearby. The court room where she shared meals with her mother was close, making her anxious to finish this routine and go. With a slap of her hand, she ordered the servants to hurry. She was hungry, and her mother was waiting.

The maidservant quickly finishes combing her long hair, straight and perfectly cut with bangs just above her eyes. They quickly grabbed her bright blue linen dress, slipping it over her head. Sandals were placed on each foot, leather straps that tied around her ankles, and wrapped up her legs to keep them sturdy as she runs, hopped or twirled.

Without a word to the servants, she turned on her heels. Golden bracelets were set into motion on her arms as she hurried to meet her mother. It was rare to see her, as Herodias was King Herod's favorite and spent most of her time away from her daughter, pleasing him. Today however, she had asked for her child to meet her.

As the food, a bowl of fruit and yogurt and a dish of cheeses, was placed before them, she drank a glass of milk, nibbling at the cheese. As they ate, her mother began to speak, informing her that the next day was the king's birthday. He had planned to share the day with his nobles, military commanders, and leading men of Galilee. There would be a great feast with plenty of meats—beef and lamb—and choice bread, fruits, and the finest wines.

"It will be wonderful," her mother shared with excitement, describing the schedule of the day's event.

The young girl squealed with delight as she was promised a finishing night of fireworks. Such fun this party would be, and she would be permitted to attend.

"Now," her mother said, reaching across the table for her hand, "you have been chosen to entertain the king with a dance."

Stunned, she stared at her mother in surprise. The biggest day of the year, the king's birthday celebration, and she would be the entertainment? She was quiet now. Her mind was racing, due in part to excitement but also sudden fear. If she were found displeasing to the king, it could be a very dangerous position. She had seen his rising anger many times around the palace, his temper causing fear in everyone. They all sought to find favor with the king.

Her mother seemed disinterested in the food before her, continuing on as if the request she had just asked of her daughter was settled. She described her daughter's costume, instructing her on how to dress, with her belt tied low, displaying her navel.

"Wear your most beautiful jewels. We have plenty. You will wear your hair loose and down, straight and shiny with oils. I have the perfect tiara that you'll wear with the prettiest stones of blue, white, and green. Remember the one King Herod gave you on your eleventh birthday?"

Mother described how to hide her face behind a veil, teasing the men in attendance by removing it only moments before she ended her dance. The veil would be enticing, draped in teeny bells and sequins, revealing only her dark eyes. Across her chest would be molded cups, where tassels and dripping jewels moved about wildly as she danced.

She had been taught this dance at a very young age, as well as many others. It seems to please her mother to learn that she knows them. Mother went on to suggest a soft pink for her dancing costume as the king wore purple, and only he could wear that rich hue in color. The pink would please him, she was told.

With the meal completed, the young girl rose to leave. But her mother grabbed her arm, twisting her around to face her, eye to eye. "You will do this and do it perfectly. It is your responsibility to please the king!"

There was no room for argument. She nodded, stepping away on trembling knees.

Turning down the hall toward her area of the palace, she found herself shaking, fighting for control. She was very aware of people outside the palace. Ever since their arrival to Jerusalem, she had heard screams, cries of the tortured from the slaves and Jews roaming the streets. King Herod was known for his hatred toward his people. She tried to block out the cries, pretending that her life was protected because of her mother's love for the king, but this morning she did not feel safe.

Arriving back in her room, she searched high and low until she found her trusted Soteria, an idol goddess that had been hers in

Greece since she was very small. She grabbed it close to her chest, yelling at a nearby servant to bring a fan and favorite candies.

She found a corner of the room where she could sit and think. Her mind was racing. Holding her small idol close, she began speaking her fears aloud: of dancing and of displeasing His Majesty the king. Fear was a tormenting spirit she had dealt with many times in her young life. Each time, Soteria had been her comfort. Murmuring to the idol, she fell asleep there in the corner, under the watchful gaze of her personal maidservant, who looked on in concern.

In the palace, everyone was at work. Cooks were in the kitchens. Fruit from the palace trees was picked, selected, polished, and situated in golden bowls for the tables of the party guests, King Herod and Herodias. Everything had to be perfect.

The pears, berries, bunches of grapes, pomegranates, apples, and kumquats were arranged in a lovely design, a handful of melon baskets artfully carved to fill with other fine delicacies. The king had a hearty appetite, and the party was expected to go long into the night.

The long tables and satin couches were made of costly fabrics, embedded in expensive jewels. Gorgeous beading and tassels decorated the dining and party-room area. Oriental rugs covered the grand, marble floors. Candles and lanterns were being placed to be lit for the celebration as evening set in. The scent of burning incense hung in the air already. The huge room where guests would be entertained was cleaned until it was spotless.

Greyhound dogs roamed the grounds. They were the king's pride and joy, one big and sleek with long legs and the other an imported Afghan hound, gorgeous creatures that the child loved.

At the maid's touch on her shoulder, she awakened, stretching as a small child. She wasn't too tall. Actually she was quite thin with long legs and a short upper waist. Glimpsing herself in the mirror, she knew she was getting close to a marriageable age. She was growing in maturity, with the women teaching things to prepare her, but she was still just a child.

Her bath was ready. This evening and into tomorrow, she

would be prepared for her entrance into the king's presence, when she would be summoned to dance for him. Fixing her hair was always hardest, with the endless drying and brushing. It must fall perfectly when she dances.

Hours later, she was put into bed, having eaten little. Her sister had brought in figs and a portion of goat cheese. They had chatted as she ate, but she could not consider her a friend. Each daughter in a royal family knew not to get too close, as they would marry other monarchs and be sent far away. It was always best to keep to yourself and play with the slave children.

The next evening had come. The palace seamstress had prepared this dance costume for just this event. It was breathtaking to behold: bangles of beautiful gold and silver hung from each thread, and yards of beautiful sheer material would appear translucent in the room lighting. The beaded bodice glittered, making her appear at least twenty years of age. She had not developed much yet at eleven, but this costume fit perfectly, enhancing her natural curves. The bottom of the harem pants blossomed out as she moved her feet. A gorgeous pink sash fell below her navel, riding low on her hips, as Herodias instructed.

The matching veil was made of the same transparent fabric as the dance harems. Chains of gold encircled her tiny waist. Her hair fell long and straight. The tiara her mother had told her about now sat upon her head, right above eyebrows darkened with black kohl. Her upper eyelids were painted with a deep-blue eye shadow with gold-colored pyrite flecks, made of ground-up lapis lazuli stone. She then darkened and lengthened her eyelashes with black kohl, a mixture of powdered lead sulfide and animal fat. Her lipstick and rouge were a mix of red ochre, a type of iron oxide clay, which the Queen of the Nile used to be known as the greatest of beauty. Every woman wanted to be beautiful like her. The young woman staring back at her looked much older than her young years.

She slid her small feet into dance slippers, pressing jewels in her nose and ears. Dozens of bracelets were brought in to choose from. She shook her head, unable to decide, so they were chosen for her and pushed onto her slender arms.

As she moved about the room, fear of the unknown gripped her, but she was determined to please the king to earn her mother's love. She was the only one she truly danced for. Just for the love of her mother.

The dance was finally complete. The king seemed pleased, both clapping and smiling. The audience followed his cue, rising and applauding. She wore a radiant smile, relieved that she had pleased the king, but her eyes sought out her mother who was laughing and applauding her on.

The king asked her to approach his throne. Quickly she climbed the steps to his side. Taking her hand, he said, "Ask anything you would be pleased with, to even half the kingdom."

She laughed to herself. *How fun! Whatever shall I ask for? A beautiful jewel? A castle of my own? Perhaps an elegant wedding dress?* These thoughts ran wildly through her mind as she descended the steps, crossing to her mother's throne.

"Mother, what should I ask?"

Her mother immediately whispered in her ear, "Ask for John the Baptist's head on a silver platter. Now!"

She was stunned at such an odd request. "Are you sure I should ask for that?"

Anger rose in her mother's face, so she quickly announced out loud, "Bring me John the Baptist's head right now on a platter!" She waited for her command to be followed.

The king looked surprised at her announcement, but because he had promised to fulfill her request, he had no choice but to do so. He sent the executioner with the orders, and because John was in the king's prison, in a very short time, the head was brought in on a platter, presented to the child.

Sickened beyond words, she took the platter and gave it to her mother. Swiftly, before anyone would notice that she had left the banquet hall, she fled the room, trembling and shaking with tears destroying her beautifully made-up face.

She hurried to her quarters, taking her anger out on the servants. "Get these clothes off me! Throw them away! Get them out of my sight quickly!"

Her servants had been running back and forth, trying to get her undressed. They caught the tiara as she flung it across the room upon entering, careful not to break the costly jewels. She ran to the waiting bath, slipping beneath the fragrant suds and covered her face, wanting to scrub away the horrid images of that head, the blood, and all she had just witnessed. She was responsible.

The maids had made ready a second pool, as this one was murky from the oils and makeup. Now she felt somewhat better, with the water warm and soothing to her spirit. She grew quiet and calm. Her heart was no longer racing. She could not speak. She was sick to her stomach. That head, jagged at the neck where he had been beheaded, haunted her thoughts. Who was he, and why had her mother demanded such a ghastly request from the king?

Again her mind wandered, recalling rumors from the streets about Jewish trouble. Had he been a part of that? Tomorrow she would find out. For now, what she needed most was rest.

Sunshine raced through the halls as she quickly went out the door at the base of the palace. She knew leaving without an escort was forbidden, but she must find the answers to her questions.

She was careful on how she dressed to fit in, to disappear into her surroundings. Last night was a nightmare of undesirable visuals, and she had to have answers. The city street was full as she searched for she knew not what. As she looked in the shops, searching the faces of the men sitting and talking, she desperately wanted to know who this man John was and why her mother had hated him so.

Rounding the corner of a sheep stall, she heard Jewish men in their traditional garb talking about a John who had been killed at the palace the following evening. This had to be him! She stepped closer, hugging the wall to keep out of sight so she could hear what they were saying. Anger was apparent to this young child. She knew that emotion and heard it in their voices. She stayed very still, with her ears straining to capture each word being spoken.

The robed men with their religious scarves of black and white discussed earnestly the death of John the Baptist. A little while into their conversation, her ears perked up as one of John's followers was mentioned, a new man, Jesus of Nazareth. She stood quietly listening when something caught her eye on the ground, a snake crawling right toward her foot. In fear she yelled out, catching the attention of the men speaking. Thinking her just a small girl, they ignored her, continuing their talk.

She ran swiftly to a grove of cool trees planted nearby, clasping her chest and murmuring a quick prayer to her goddess. Trying to figure everything out is hard when you are not part of the outside world, but just the mention of this man, Jesus, and her heart had been pierced. Amazed, she pondered his name. What was the connection?

It was now the end of August. The party, etched in her mind forever, had taken place on the twenty-ninth of August in AD 28. Her childish laughter and fun were now gone; anger, confusion, and bitterness were finding their way into the tiny heart of this small child running through the streets of Jerusalem.

She was not aware of time, but hunger has a way of catching up to you, and hungry she was. No coins were ever needed in the palace, so she had nothing with which to buy food. Looking around, she decided to make her way back to where she came from. Catching her breath, she began her journey, hopeful for rest and something to eat. Her mind was still full of questions.

The servants had searched all day to find her, never speaking a word to anyone for fear of losing their heads. In terror, they searched every section of the palace where she might have escaped to. They knew how distraught she had been from the beheading, as they were too.

Throughout the palace, there was much gossip among the servants who were very aware of who this John was. He was named Baptist due to immersing people in water, when their sins were given to God, a very new thing coming from a group called the Essenes, who did this for cleansing. John preached forgiveness of sin and showed immersion as washing away their sins.

When she entered the sitting area in the room where she slept, you could almost hear an audible sigh of relief ripple through the princess's quarters. Swiftly she was placed in a pool of water, which she was grateful for, but her mind wandered off as the servants scrubbed her feet and hair. They were mindful of the dust that came from city streets but did not dare question her whereabouts.

She was lifted from one pool to another for the oils and pampering, soothing her for rest. A plate of cheese, wafers, fruits, and nuts was brought to her, which she ate hungrily. She was exhausted from running the streets, trying to stay out of sight while at the same time desperate to find out more about this man, John. Overwhelmed, she finally succumbed to the power of sleep, a deep sleep with no thoughts or dreams. It was just the peaceful, content sleep of a child.

Her maid, in a bed close by, watched as she slept, knowing that something had taken place. She had cared for this child since she was born. She had wet-nursed her as a babe, rocked her to sleep, dressed and bathed her, laughed with her at play, and applauded the first steps she had taken.

When troubled, the maid knew how her eyes would scrunch up as she tried to figure out the situation at hand, but tonight as she watched the child, she found her at peace. Tomorrow would bring fresh news, but for now, the quarters were quiet as peace settled over this part of the palace.

Laziness seemed to have found a partner as the sun rose, shooting across the room, catching a crystal prism, and twirling rainbows of light across the room. A soft breeze stirred the pendant into constant motion as the girl awakened, stretching her legs and arms. She smiled at the dancing rainbows. Such beauty. Watching the movement of color in appreciation, she felt a calming peace as her eyes followed the rainbows.

The sun moved on, and so must she. Her servant girl rushed to her side to help her into the robe and night shoes as she stepped toward her bath. She smiled without exchanging words with the servants.

She rose from the bath a short time later; the servants dressed her in beautiful garments. She sat quietly as they combed her hair, placing beautiful combs painted with pretty birds and pulling back tousled curls from her face.

Strolling down the hall toward the courtroom for a light breakfast, she noticed a lizard quickly run up the stone wall just as a spider came into view. Her eyes took it all in. It happened so quickly. As the spider was caught, the lizard moved on in its morning search for more breakfast. She giggled and took her seat at the table to be served her favorite breakfast—yogurt, fruit, almonds, and milk for her young body.

It was a quiet meal, as there was no one to talk to. At this time of day, she would go over what she needed to do. Yesterday, she had gone in search of what she wanted to know, but she knew there was more. Now she questioned herself, *What is it I want to know?*

Dance class wasn't until the afternoon, so the morning was hers to do with as she pleased, but she didn't like her choices of reading, painting, and needlework. None of that sounded remotely fun. She picked at the fruit and took a bite of yogurt, realizing she wasn't hungry after all. Leaving her untouched breakfast, she snuck down the back steps of the palace once again, finding herself on the city streets.

This time she was not dressed to blend in, so she kept watch of her surroundings, knowing she could be recognized. Careful to stay in the shadows as much as possible, she listened.

The men were again speaking in a group. She tried to get close enough to hear but not be seen. She watched them intently in their black robes, wrapped in the traditional black-and-white striped scarves they wore. Their headdresses must depend on rank because they were different.

They were not so angry today as they discussed the new man again, this man from Galilee, Jesus. It seemed from their talk that they were curious about him, being baptized by John in the river, and now there were people following him instead.

As she turned to leave the area where the Pharisee men had gathered, among the crowd came a good deal of noise. Quickly running down the street to see what had caused the commotion, she saw masses of people pushing and shoving. Their expressions were jubilant as they pushed forward, trying to get closer to something or someone.

And there he was. A man easily noticed, his commanding presence caused the multitude to press in closer. With her being so tiny, she could easily sneak in between the robes and skirts, now right on the edge of the crowd where he would pass by. As he came closer, the crowd pressed toward him with outstretched arms, hoping just to touch him.

His eyes were mesmerizing, piercing, and sharp. He stopped right in front of her. Compassion filled his gaze as he touched a poor man kneeling at his feet, as if to a king. She hardly dared to breathe as she stood quiet and still, wanting to touch this man too, but she was afraid, for now he had gone down the road with the throng of people following.

She walked over to a tree, a short distance away. *His name is Jesus*, she told herself, hearing the cries of the people as they called out His name. This man was John's friend. What was it about Him that made her want to know Him more? Who was He who walked the streets of Jerusalem, drawing all these people that caused the robed men to speak of him as well?

After a while, feeling hunger pains, she realized once again that it was getting late and she needed to return home. After a warm bath and soothing massage, hair combed and readied for bed, she rested and waited for the servants to bring her some food. Eating alone each night was a regular practice for her. She liked it, quite frankly. The servant girl cared for her very much, and she was quiet company.

After she had eaten, she asked if anyone had noticed that she had missed her dance class and was relieved that no one had. No one had come looking for her. She finished her snacks and crawled into the bed that was large enough for an elephant to sleep with her. She smiled. *What a thought, an elephant.* Giggling to herself, she snuggled down into the covers and slept.

Sunshine was bright as she pressed against the walls in the shadows, trying to miss the rays of light that shot through the windows. After one flight of steps, she would be out! A guard passed at the very moment. She made a move to sneak out. *Whoa! Close call*, she thought. She stayed right against the wall, hoping he would keep walking.

Peeking around the corner, she saw him disappear out of sight, providing just enough time to try for an escape. *Zoom!* Past the gardens of flowers, she paused to marvel at their beauty this time of year. She went past the palace gates and headed to the streets yet again.

Today she was on a mission. On this third day, she had to find Jesus. It was a must. But where would she find this man? The streets were quieter this early in the morning. The black-robed men seemed intent on something in their group, but she paid them no mind. Finding Jesus was her pursuit.

Turning a corner, she saw Him, surrounded by men in colorful robes. Others sat a short distance away; others were standing. All were listening. Jesus was sitting on the stump of a fallen tree as he talked to the crowd that had come. She was just about to move forward when a group of children ran to him. He accepted them gladly, so she followed behind them.

One of the men grabbed at her arm, trying to hold her back, but Jesus stopped him. Jesus called the children to him and said, "Let the little children come to me, and do not hinder them, for the kingdom of God belongs to such as these" (Luke 18:16 NIV).

Jesus reached out to touch her, laughing with great joy as he held out his arms to gather the children to himself. She had never had a hug before and had never felt such love before. Her eyes filled with tears while looking at Him. He was telling the children how much He loved them and how wonderful they each were, and then He blessed them! She gasped, hearing His words. He was telling them, the children, that the kingdom of heaven was theirs. A feeling she had never experienced before flooded her, touching her deeply. Tears ran down her face, touching her heart. Life would never be the same again, no matter what, she decided.

Laughing and smiling, the children clung to Him. He invited them to sit at His feet as He spoke to them. She too sat and listened, unable to take her eyes off Him. She wanted nothing more than to stay there, listening to Him speak. How she loved Him! His words were spoken with such authority that even the men were in awe of His presence as she was. *Who was this man called Jesus?* she wondered.

Quietly, she got up, going to the back of the crowd, toward a semicircle of people, noting something of interest. Groups of women were also standing off to the side, listening as He spoke, and one woman looked exactly like Him. She must be His mother, she guessed.

A few of the children had gotten up, kissing His cheek as they left, but a few remained. Their wide-eyed gazes were fixed on His face as He spoke. Happy smiles were all around. The ladies noticed her. One of them smiled as she held out her hand in invitation. She had been standing there, unsure of what to do next, but as the lady's hand was extended, she took it, joining their group.

Quietly now, they stood together. For a moment, she held onto the lady's hand, but as the women nodded to each other, they began to move away to prepare the food. The woman who looked like Jesus lingered behind.

"Are you hungry, child?"

"Oh, yes please," she replied.

"Come and help prepare a lunch for the Master, and you may eat," the lady offered.

The young girl's heart swelled at the thought of doing something, anything, for Jesus. She placed the napkins and bowls where she was directed. Plenty of food was available. In a few moments, Jesus was asked to announce that it was time to gather and eat.

She was thrilled to pass the bowls of fruits, vegetables, and chunks of bread around to those present, the men eating hungrily, laughing, and talking among themselves. She kept her eyes on Jesus, glancing between Him and His mother to see her reaction as He spoke. She saw such laughter and experienced such joy in their company.

It was getting late. She should return to the palace before dinner would be served. She was struck by the peace and calm that was over everyone there. As she turned to go, she knew in her heart that she was His beloved child. Life ceased being the same the moment He came into her heart. She felt such peace, no longer bound up in fear. She felt such joy without any of the worries she used to carry. Jesus had made her childish heart so happy. Joy was new to her as a beloved follower of Jesus.

CHALK TALK

Pure
Matthew 5:8; Psalm 139:24; Psalm 24:4–5; Proverbs 16:2

Love
1 Corinthians 16:14; Romans 13:8; Proverbs 4:23

Pleasing
Galatians 1:10; Romans 8:8; 1 John 3:22; Psalm 19:4

Fear
Psalm 56:3; 2 Timothy 1:7; Isaiah 35:4; Psalm 55:22

Joy
Matthew 18:3; 1 Peter 3:4

Vengeance
Deuteronomy 32:35; 1 Thessalonians 5:15; 1 Samuel 24:12

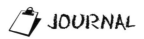 **JOURNAL**

Have you been so curious that you searched until you found the answer? Are you curious for information and answers to things you may not understand? Write your biggest challenge and how you would solve it with your inquisitive mind.

Joann Jordan

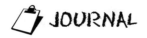 JOURNAL

THE SACRIFICE

JUDGES 11

She was standing in the window, watching and wondering as the sun blazed over the hills. It was going to be a great day. With a trace of a grin on her face and a flick of her long, dark hair, she began to hum. This was that day of excitement that her family had been waiting for. Looking around to find just the right sash and sandals, she tugged at her long skirt and, with speed, tied and wrapped the sash into place. She had made this skirt for just this moment from the flax her mother had brought home. She had begun cleaning and weaving it a while ago. Sometimes she would daydream because the weaving was so repetitive, causing her to have to tear back and restart. This time, the skirt was very special, and it had to be perfect.

Her dad was coming home from the war a hero. Rumors were all over the village of Gilead that he was Israel's champion. Victory was his because he was a warrior. Yahweh had given them victory over their enemies, and today she would lead the dancing and singing as they celebrated his return. It was a glorious day. Her heart was happy for the father she loved. She knew how important this assignment had been. He had been given the chance to lead an army of Israelites against the heathen Ammonites, a very big and prestigious appointment, and now he would be coming home victorious, sitting high on his stallion in beautiful armor.

She moved about the room checking the dance steps, with

her skirt swirling as she lifted each foot lightly, toe to heel. Her heart felt huge with joy because the days of celebration were very near. Listening for the hoofbeats of horses, she was aware it was almost time.

Jephthah had been born of a prostitute his father had taken in a drunken state one night while attending a party. The men had gathered together celebrating nothing special, but because of his actions, the prostitute became pregnant, acting on her rights to demand care of his child, a son. Jephthah was not accepted as an Israelite because his mother was a heathen Moabite, much hated for their idol worship and child sacrifice. A mother's nationality determined their place in society, so his burden was twofold: one of prostitution and the other being declared a Moabite, his mother's son instead of his father's. His father had married a woman with whom he had more sons legally. When they were grown, they forced him to leave Gilead, as they didn't want to share their inheritance with him.

This wasn't news in her house. The family had always known their history. Her father wasn't ashamed of himself, but more of his father, who had not protected his firstborn son.

Today would be different. In the days and years to come, her father would be known as a great warrior hero, recognized by the whole village of Israelites. Flushed and humming, twisting and turning, she waited for help with her long hair that glistened in the sunlight. Just then, her mother entered, bringing beautiful, hand-painted combs to pull back and fasten her dark ringlets. Curly wisps would fall into her face as she danced, unless they were restrained. Comb in her hand and speaking softly, her mother questioned her on the choice of songs, laughing with delight at her selection and joining her with singing.

The ladies of the village had gathered outside, waiting for her. They were dressed in beautiful colors of celebration; bright scarves covered their hair. Belt buckles shone in the sunshine like stars as the women practiced their welcome dance that she would soon lead them into. Now into their homes they scurried. It was the daughter's honor to be the first to greet the warrior. She would burst through the door, leading them all in loud song, clasping the tambourine as it jingled, smiles on all the faces.

She waited. Galloping hoofbeats were heard in the distance. The sound of running across the sands caused the group to begin circling so the victor's daughter could come flying out the door of her home, twirling and dancing as she jingled the tambourine, and singing loudly the songs of praise!

> Oh, victory is yours, our hero, champion for Israel today. We dance and sing joyfully as you receive your fair share salute over our enemies. Yahweh has blessed you, O victor, and glory is surrounding you, Israel's leader. We dance and sing for generations to come, of the mighty hand of God who has given such courage and handed the blessing to us.

And there he was, sitting high on his black stallion, wearing the dress of a warrior. The sun gleamed off his armor and shield that now rested in his belt sash. The horse stopped as he pulled on the reins, making his descent. Looking up at that moment, he heard his daughter's cry of excitement as she stepped out the door of her house. She twirled, danced, and sang loudly the songs of Israel's glory, God's gracious victory for her father.

She ran to be gathered into his arms, stopping short at the sight of her father on the ground. He was bent over on one knee, appearing to be weeping. She approached him timidly now, knowing something was terribly wrong. He reached for her hand, howling like a wounded animal. Pain crossed his weathered face. Fear clenched her heart. *Oh, what is wrong? What mystery is this?* she thought. What could be so wrong that her father would hold her hand tightly, howling loudly as he wept? She stood very still.

Youth has little knowledge of good and evil. In that moment, she felt as young as a baby, at a loss to what had just happened. The excited young girl who had stepped through the door leading the ladies into celebration now found herself a small child, standing before the father she adored, speechless and frightened. Was she somehow responsible for his grief?

She knelt too, and he grabbed her close, crushing her to him. Sorrow that should have been joy had now caused her to become frightful. Her mother had come dancing with all the others and now separated herself, stepping forward to touch his shoulder. He stood up, still holding their girl in his arms, and she could feel his pain.

Quietly he asked for them all to leave, thanking them as he carried his daughter. His wife followed back into the house. He put her down on the floor, sitting on a stool reserved for him.

The room was awash in colored scarves and lettering of congratulations. Candles glowed in every corner; sweet fragrances floated in the air. A carefully planned meal was prepared, chosen for the victor, Jephthah. His beloved wife had thoughtfully put together his favorite foods. Now he shook his head, wanting nothing. The room was quiet; no one was speaking.

It seemed as if an eternity had passed before he lifted his head. Mother's face wore tears, bearing an expression of concern. The young girl stepped away and sat on another stool, just a short distance from her father as he began to speak. With words of grief, he explained that the war had been hard. The enemy Ammonites were many, surrounding them as his men were wounded and killed in battle. He had felt that what he thought could be accomplished swiftly was now becoming a truly dangerous defeat, impossible if he had not had Yahweh on his side.

He spoke boldly now, more confident, as he explained what took place on the battlefield, his need for Yahweh's help. He stopped his story to ask for water, which the servants quickly brought. After a long drink, he continued. In one desperate moment on the battlefield, he had made a horrible decision to challenge Yahweh. "If He would rescue us, give us victory over the enemy, I would in turn sacrifice."

Now his voice dropped so low in tone that Mother bent forward to hear his words. His daughter watched his lips as they uttered the next sentence, "I told God that the first to come out the door of my home when we returned, I would offer to Him as a sacrifice." It was a horrible, hideous oath to Yahweh.

No one moved. Mother gasped with her hand over her mouth. She moaned as tears rained down her face. The child sat very still and quiet on the stool. She was young in age, young in spirit, but she had known Yahweh all her life. Her mother had told her the wonderful stories of Abraham, Isaac, and Jacob and the wars of triumph that Israel had waged to keep the land that God had given His people. She had heard about the mighty warriors' victories and blessings that God had bestowed upon His chosen people, powerful stories she had been instructed to learn and pass down to her children once she married and had her own family.

Yahweh was great. Other gods in the village she had seen often; her friends had strange idols made by human hands. It seemed odd that you could worship and pray to something you could make yourself. It was easy for her to believe her mother's beautiful stories. It just made sense in a young mind. The air she breathed and the skies filled with the purest of white clouds. Her mother had said that high in the heavens, beyond what she could see, lived the God she prayed to.

Now she sat, thinking of that God and the vow her father had made. The first to come out of the house, he would sacrifice. She was that one. Quiet loomed over the room. Father just sat there, looking off as if words mattered not, shaking his head as if to say "no … no …" But his statement in the room had stifled all joy, peace, energy, and victory from those who were present. Everyone remained silent.

Thoughtfully, she left her stool and went to her father. Lifting his head with her small hand, she brushed the hair back from his eyes. In a quiet whisper, she told him that Yahweh would understand that she was willing to be the covenant sacrifice. She was a faithful child, raised to honor God, obey her parents, and surrender all things to the One who created her and everything she had ever seen. Again, she let him know that she was willing to follow through on his promise to God.

Amazement flashed across his face. Her mother gasped,

catching her breath as her child smiled, offering herself as a willing sacrifice. If it were His choice to receive her, as her father had pledged, then let it be so.

Again, silence as thick as the air on a humid day filled the room before her father spoke. He requested her to choose anything she would like to do before she gave her life. Unable to reply, she asked to talk tomorrow and think over her decision. In the quiet, she walked over to the room where she slept, passing by the beautiful hangings and drapes to prepare for prayer.

In the village of Gilead, heroes in the other homes ate, talked, and wondered about the most unusual welcome they had just witnessed. A war hero was rejoiced, sung to, and danced for with love by all the people for the victory they had won. The men had traveled a long way from the battlefront and spent nights sleeping under the stars, drinking and celebrating their victory among themselves. There was a lot of congratulatory slaps across the back and arm-wrestling to ward off the excitement of finally winning triumph over tough adversity. They enjoyed these moments as men do, collectively giving praise to one another for the battle that had been won. Even though no one knew how, they just thought it was their strength and mobility.

So tonight in each of their homes, they were honored by their families and served by servants. They thought it strange how the victory singing and dancing had been called off by Jephthah and how he had seemed shocked by seeing his young daughter dance toward him as they rode up. Their wives were also curious, as all women are. At Jephthah's instruction, the women who were singing and dancing had stopped, looking over their shoulders at the victor with his child, unable to hear their words.

When they asked their husbands about it, they had no answers. The crowd that had gathered to celebrate broke up into individual homes. The gossip continued at their tables. Night came, and sleep was easy now that their soldiers were back in their beds with family safely beside them. They had earned this blissful night of needed sleep. And rest they did.

But not Jephthah. He could not sleep. He was pacing back and forth, trying to lie down but unable to rest. He tossed and turned until finally in exasperation, he went out to walk toward the hills outside of Gilead.

He found himself prostrate on the ground, speaking out loud, quietly but audibly, to the God of the universe, the God who made the stars and the moon he was witnessing this night. He told Yahweh how much he appreciated the victory over the Ammonites, how he knew that He had given him the victory. He confessed what a terrible mistake it was to promise God a person for a sacrifice.

Jephthah didn't know as much as his wife of the great men and women of generations past, or the real reason why Israel was called the chosen people. He did know with great fear how Yahweh took an oath to be binding and, if broken, He damned generations even to death.

Now he rose, pleading for mercy not to kill his only child, lamenting before his Creator to take back his pledge but hearing nothing. The sun was rising over the eastern skies as Jephthah moved from his place of exhaustion, looking upward once again to ask for mercy.

Across the village, sounds of pans and fires started for cooking and well as water being carried by the servants could be heard. He identified smells in the air as households came to life. He entered his home to find hanging pots of water ready to cook the eggs, soups, vegetables, and grains left over from their uneaten dinner the night before.

Seeing that he was hungry now, his wife wordlessly began to prepare a plate to eat and water and wine to drink. Cheese was a favorite, and pomegranate was a special treat, which she placed at his right hand for him to take and enjoy. He looked at her, still not speaking but consuming the hearty meal with gusto.

From her room, the young girl appeared, walking in to touch her father's shoulder. She leaned down to kiss his cheek. The look on his face was one of surprise and full of gratitude. As she sat down, she greeted her parents, asking if she might speak.

At her father's nod, she told them what had taken place the night before, when she had gone to her room. She had been unconcerned, yet she'd had no answers for what her father had revealed to them of his covenant with Yahweh. She had thanked Him for His protection, her father's victory against the Ammonites, and peace for the Israelites, grateful that her father was safely home. She also knew that Yahweh would provide a way to help her father in his pain over words he should not have spoken.

As she spoke, her parents had stopped eating to listen. She told them of her reminder to God, that her father didn't mean child sacrifice as the Moabites did, but that she would present herself a living sacrifice to God. Her father, raised by a Moabite woman, did not understand that Yahweh would not accept human sacrifices.

"I offered myself to Yahweh in my prayers last night," she continued. "I understand that my life is to be alone, to serve my family and community."

She would never marry or have little ones of her own but would help mothers across Gilead or wherever she was needed. She would stay celibate and pure, trusting God to care for her, providing what she would earn in helping others. She would have her own place, a tent or small place to sleep, separated from her family to carry out what she felt was God's will. Her mother turned away with tears coming. It frustrated her husband when she cried.

Her father, without a word, held open outstretched arms to his daughter, and she went to him. He lifted her onto his knee, putting his hand through her beautiful hair, his eyes also filling with tears. *How could such a young child have such an old soul?* he wondered to himself. Yet here she was, speaking as if she were a grown adult about the ways of Yahweh and the decision she felt she would carry out, according to his pledge to God.

He hugged her close to his chest. "If you are willing to surrender your life in this way, so be it." Relief was his not to have to sacrifice his daughter as the Moabites did, piercing her with a burning sword. He stood up, swinging her into a dance step. Laughter filled the room; joy spread across his face. Mother too had stopped crying, realizing that God had provided a solution to a very difficult situation. She joined them in laughter of joy. Her daughter's life had been spared!

Now the joy that should have been yesterday's filled the house, falling out into the streets. Her father stopped twirling his daughter, setting her on the floor. With a kiss on her forehead, he asked if there were anything that he could give her. She nodded. Her request was simple. In a week, she would be fourteen. She would like to go away with her friends for a two-month period of time and celebrate her dedication of celibacy and service to God before beginning her life of solitude.

Her parents were stunned but agreed. They would speak with the other parents, explain the situation, and grant their permission for her friends to join her. While she was gone, her father said he would build her a home that she could live in, where she could cook and have friends visit. It could also be used as a place to care for someone in need. Everyone seemed content with the plan.

A few days later, twelve young women from Gilead, with sacks of food and clothing, set off for the mountains. Tiny, white flowers in full bloom filled the trees and grass. The girls were full of excitement. Joy and happiness were apparent on their faces as they danced together, arm in arm. They may have been starting a new tradition in Israel, as this had never been done before. The hills above Gilead require a day's journey to climb, but the girls were young and full of energy. Such freedom they felt away from work in the home baking bread or weaving.

Once they had reached the top, where none had ever been, it was even more beautiful and thrilling. The day was getting late, so they spread blankets to rest, kneeled to say their nightly prayers, bowed before the eastern sky, and thanked Yahweh for safety up the mountain.

They lay back, watching the stars as they twinkled across the sky and gasping in delight as a long-tailed comet vanished out of sight, leaving them in awe of their Creator. Designs formed before their eyes in the heavens. Her friends, with dreamy eyes, talked of their future weddings and longings for a happy home with their husbands someday, but she felt peace in her commitment to serve Yahweh.

The days ahead were filled with gaiety, laughter, dancing,

and singing. They swapped stories of childhood, sharing their deepest dreams and biggest hopes. Each morning they woke with thankfulness to Yahweh, closing out each evening with grateful hearts for this freedom and joy that they had never experienced before. Time passed.

It was time to begin their descent down the mountain. They began gathering their bags together to return to their village. Bonds of friendship that would last a lifetime had been forged during those two months. With hugs, kisses, and promises, they began their journey back. Even now, each knew they had changed. They had gone up the mountain as girl-children, but they were coming home as young women.

Several years passed since this historical account. Now, Jephthah's daughter had her special place in the village. She had become a folk heroine to many. She was invited to all her friends' weddings, helping to mend, design, or dress the bride. She had watched children being born as she learned to be a helpmate and midwife. She had made herself available to lend a hand where needed, sometimes in the home her father had built her.

When her father and her friend's fathers had passed on into paradise, she too had begun to feel weary but content. Her God faithfully answered the prayers that she prayed throughout her lifetime. Yahweh, who gives all things and knows all things, had been her rock and shield. Morning and evening she had offered herself to Him, worshipping His name, thankful for His goodness. Life was peaceful in His will.

 CHALK TALK

Shiela

The Bible does not give us the name of Jephthah's daughter, but she is called Sheila by Jewish rabbis. Each year in early spring, the young women will spend four days celebrating her life. She is still honored for her willingness to present her life and be a living sacrifice to God. Her actions show that a promise made to God must be kept and that honoring one's parents finds favor in the eyes of God. Her story also demonstrates that friendship among women is very important, and it is also important to be a help to the community and a worshipper of God.

One life given is always remembered two thousand years later.

She was busy preparing herself (Proverbs 12:24). She honored her mother and father (Exodus 20:12). She surrendered to God her needs (Isaiah 25:1). She prayed for guidance (Proverbs 3:5–6).

She listened (Proverbs 16:20). She included others (Proverbs 13:20). She shared her concerns with friends (Proverbs 11:25). She made her decision based on faith (Psalm 19:8).

Warrior and Judge

Jephthah had to have his ego enriched. He was hasty (Proverbs 21:5). He promised to God a covenant (Ecclesiastes 5:4). He was foolish with pride (Proverbs 14:3). He took glory at the cost of others (Proverbs 16:16). He lost his chance at a heritage carrying on his name (Isaiah 42:8). He was not a hero but a zero (Proverbs 15:27; Judges 11:1).

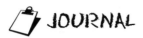 **JOURNAL**

Did it bother you that the father was willing to give up someone else's life so he could be recognized and given power over others? The story of this young person could be anyone in our world today. As you read the story and scripture, what do you think caused the person to approach a better solution than the original decision? Journal how you would have worked through a life-or-death situation that seemed to have no hope.

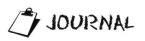 JOURNAL

THE SLAVE

---

2 KINGS 5

It was spring in northern Israel and warm. Not a breeze was in the air. The children, searching for a cool place to play, giggled and whispered in each other's ears unknown secrets that only children share. As they were trying to decide what they should do this warm, sunny day, one suggested they go to the water where it was cool and where there were many trees for shade. The children, rousing and joyfully singing the songs of childhood, walked, skipped, and ran to the river's edge. They took off their sandals and waded in the cool water of Pharos.

Her dark-red hair was tied up today. A cute pin held most of it off her face so she would be free of it falling into her face. She occasionally blew her breath across the tresses of hair, when it would fall and cover her right eye. After a slap to her face, it would go back into the other tangles that her mother had tried to control this morning before she went out the door of her home.

Caution was the instruction from her poppa that morning, reminding her that they could be invaded, as spring had arrived and the time for the raids was coming. She had laughed at her poppa with her childlike joy, which made her poppa smile as he patted her on her shoulder.

Following the others by removing her sandals, she stepped into the water. It was indeed cold. She was yelping and jumping up and down as the splashing and laughter grew louder. Yelling at the silliness of the children was a joy. Anyone coming upon this sight could not help but smile. Such joy was displayed in having a delightful time, as only children know how to do.

Her hair kept falling over her eyes, and finally in exasperation, she pulled out the pins holding it and allowed the thick, red, curly hair to fall down past her shoulders. Her poppa loved her golden-red locks and often requested that she release it so he could admire her beauty. Her mother wore a festive scarf over her reddish hair so it stayed off her face as she worked, but she was not required to do so. Therefore loose curls were often let free instead of being tied up now and then, as they had been today.

Finally after playing in the water, hanging from branches of the trees that tempted the kids to swing from them, they began to put their sandals back on and prepared to return home. Refreshed by the water and laughter of friends, they now were needing nourishment. *Children are forever hungry, growing so quickly as they do, especially boys*, she thought, smiling.

She was just about eight and didn't crave food like her brother, who was older and was, as their mother said with a laugh, never full. She turned, ready to get up, when she heard a sound an inch away! A hand grabbed her at the waist and picked her up.

Stunned, she yelled and felt fear before she could see. The twisting of her body gave way to the force of this person who held her up almost above his head. He yelled that he had a redheaded girl and then placed her on his shoulder, upside down, so she couldn't see his face or come to her senses. She must have screamed, but she was so frightened that she couldn't tell what she had done.

He was running with her, and she couldn't see anything as her head bounced off his back. Terror was all she could feel right now. Thoughts were numb. She was so frightened that she couldn't comprehend anything. Fear does that. It locks down your senses.

This man now threw her onto the front of his saddle, and he climbed on behind her. Wiping the tears she didn't even know she was shedding from her eyes, she tried to comprehend what had happened. Seeing the men in front of her on their horses and her two other friends crying as they too were taken by force, she let her eyes search to see who was with this group of raiders, hoping one would be her brother. It was not. Instead, there were two boys a little older than she was but still part of the group of her friends. She stopped crying and tried to decide if she could jump that far without breaking her leg or foot. She decided she was too little to do that.

As they rode across the border of Israel on the northeastern side of the mountain, her fear increased, knowing that these enemies tortured and sacrificed children. She recognized that might be her fate. This man did not speak to her. He rode like a warrior, confident, and sat high in his saddle. His headdress was a symbol of his position—silver covered with a high plume of red feathers and insignias that pointed to his position in the military. That caused her even greater concern.

He dismantled the horse and told her to stay as he wandered off into the woods. She did not move. The others were surrounding them, and she knew she could not get away. Reason told her that her brother had gone home and advised her parents of what had happened.

As he returned, the man gazed up at her. She moved her head, and she too stared at her captor. By this time, she was really hungry, and he spoke to her, asking if she would like a piece of bread and cheese. She nodded, and quickly from his saddle, he handed her enough to stop the aching of her tummy. He gazed at her with eyes that looked kind, but she knew that wasn't possible. No kind person steals another man's child. He was looking at her with an inquisitive gaze. She stared at him too. Perplexed, she felt uncomfortable but sat up as straight as she could as she straddled the horse.

Much later, entering a large guarded gate, it looked as if there were two or three hundred men on horses. The man's horse led the way. She had a good idea he was very important. Sounds of excitement greeted the raiders as they came into the square of their city. People everywhere wanted to see what trophies they had brought back. It was, after all, the first raid of the season, and the townspeople knew much more would follow. "Only three children were brought," said a man to another. "Not much on this venture, but more to come."

She was terrified by now. The people were staring at her, and she had no idea what was to happen. Again she thought of how she had heard they killed and sacrificed children. Would she be their gift to the gods they served? She whispered a prayer to her God, Jehovah. "Help me, oh Jehovah."

Moments passed, and then the man jumped back on his saddle and took her to a castle sitting at the far end of the town. The long road seemed never-ending, and they went across a bridge of water that roared and hit hard against the stone that held it within boundaries. She was scared. Horns blew as they approached. The man sat up very straight in his armor, and she was terrified. Who was this man? Was he the king? Questions were racing through her head as he approached a group of many people who gathered outside the huge doors adorned with a very large emblem on each side. The people cheered and waved, and horns with banners blew as they came through the doors into the courtyard filled with beautiful flowers and baby sheep. Flowers and sheep made her think that maybe he wasn't too mean. *Maybe he will not sacrifice me? Maybe?*

He dismounted and grabbed her again, lifting her down from the horse. She was wobbly because she had not walked for hours, and she was again hungry and thirsty. He led her into the area of the house where she could see lots of people working and cooking. The aroma of the food was about to make her faint when he ordered a big, stout lady to give her food and water. The bowl was set before her, and she drank the water so fast that the woman laughed and refilled the glass.

This time she sipped at it but picked up her spoon to eat the bowl of thick soup in front of her. The woman laid a thick piece of bread in front of her like the one her captor had given her when they were coming here. Hunger overtook thoughts, and she ate.

Silence can be a gift, and right now silence was what she needed to clear her head and quiet her mind from fear. She allowed her mother's teachings to seep in and her trust in Jehovah to come forward. She needed to remember she was an Israelite, the child of the tribes, and Jehovah knew where and why she was here. "Do not fear," she had been told. "God is our strength, and He will care for His people." As she ate, these thoughts raced through her mind.

The woman came over and took her empty bowl, and she finished the water. Now she waited and looked around, seeing strange things like huge cooking pots, three or four times bigger than those at her home. This area had hanging fruits and vegetables like her mother did; some she recognized and others she did not know. Her mother had been training her to know such things, and work in the kitchen had been a new job to her, but she was not yet allowed around the fire because she was too young, her poppa had said.

A cot was ready for her, and the woman took her down a long hall in this big castle and told her to sleep there. Terror crept over her again, as only a candle glowed in the hall and she could not see anything around her. Tears fell down her cheeks as she tried to control the cries from escaping her mouth. Who might hear her, and was someone else in this space with her? No nightclothes were given to her, and there was no washbasin to wash the grime of the road off her face and hands. Trembling, she bent over to get on the cot, hoping for a cloth to cover with. There was none.

Morning came, and the sun shined as if nothing had happened to her. She pushed her tiny body to the side of the cot, and looking around in the dimness of the room, she saw another two cots, empty but off against another wall away from hers. They had covers, so she thought she might ask for one too before night came again.

She stood up and ventured to the door, looking right and left, not sure which way she had come from. Around the corner, way down the left hall, the woman came. She looked as if she might have clothes or a robe with her. She stopped right in front of her and ordered her to follow.

Fear is a strong power. It will cause you to stop thinking and just react. She was afraid but followed her as ordered down the hall on the right side of the door she'd left. As they came closer, the woman inquired about her needing the bath. She would need to wash her hair and prepare herself for the master. The child nodded and looked to see who else might be around. She saw no one. She slipped off her dress and went into the warm pool of water.

The woman had left, and now she returned, handing her clean clothing, undergarments, and a blue robe with a brown sash. Her hair was still drying, and the woman took a large comb from her pocket and began to comb her red locks. She was kind and very careful, as the child had curly hair and it tangled easily. When they were finished, she gave her sandals and instructed her to follow.

Breakfast was good, and hunger can replace fear. She welcomed the food that was given to her—yogurt and bread with fruit. So good. Now she was taken up steps to the second and third floor and into a large, beautiful room. She looked around and was left there by herself. The woman disappeared.

A door opened behind her, and she turned to see that the man was standing there, looking at her. She trembled. Thoughts ran through her mind, and fear showed on the child's face. She breathed a prayer. Tears came, and the man crossed the large room and towered over her. He handed her a cloth, and she wiped her face. As he did so, she noticed spots on his hand, oddly shaped and ugly.

He informed her to follow him, and he walked across the room to the door. He opened it, and she walked into a large room with a huge bed and a lady sitting up in the bed, looking at him and the child.

He quickly informed the lady that he had brought her a gift from his raid. She was the gift. The child was quiet. The lady looked at her and laughed, so tiny but loved, she with the beautiful red hair. The child was told to come closer, and the lady reached out, touched her, and moved her hand over her hair, exclaiming with delight, her love of the gift, this child.

Time passed. The tears and loneliness from missing your mother, poppa, and even your brother never go away. She was ten now. She kept a calendar at her tiny desk in the room next to her mistress. Her bed was nice, and she had nice garments chosen for her. She was allowed to bathe daily, and washing and dressing well were important to the lady. And so she was careful to be very clean and fresh.

She did as her mistress instructed, and her routine was to run errands and serve her breakfast from the kitchen, brought up at sunrise. As the mistress bathed, she made her bed, refreshing the sheet by sprinkling lavender and salts and then brushing them off. She cleared the chest and arranged fresh flowers in pots around the room, making sure the reflection glass was clean so her mistress could see herself when she returned from her bath. She cleaned the combs and brushes, as each day, three times for sure, she brushed the mistress's hair.

Today as the mistress returned, she seemed bothered. She sat down, and the child knew exactly what to do. She took the creams and rubbed it onto her arms and then her legs and feet. Then she took the brush and comb. She began the process of preparing her hair. The lady was troubled. The child was quiet.

Finally the mistress spoke. "If only there were a cure for leprosy. He is getting worse now and soon will not be able to be around others."

The child listened. Quietly she inquired if she may speak. Her mistress said yes. The child told her about a prophet in Israel who could heal leprosy if he would go to him. Her mistress jumped up and said to wait. She went away, and now the child thought, *Oh dear, I am in trouble. They hate Israelites.*

Just as she was fearing for her life, the lady returned with Naaman. "Tell him what you said to me," she demanded.

She explained to her master about Elisha, the prophet of God, and how all Israel knew he could ask Jehovah to heal someone and it was done. She said she believed if he would travel to Israel and talk to Elisha, he would be healed of his leprosy.

From the window, she watched as her master left in his chariot with his team of men on horses to go into Samaria and find Elisha. The child was concerned. If Elisha could not heal him, it could mean her death, but she believed in Jehovah's power to heal her master and that Elisha would do it. Her faith was strong.

As he entered the city, he went straight to the king with the letter given to him by the king of Aran. As he handed him the letter, the king screamed with fear and tore his garments. Terrified, he realized this warrior thought he, the king, could heal him. With great anguish, he explained that he was not God and could heal no one. News reached Elisha, and he told his servant to get the man from Aran and bring him to his place.

As the commander of the Aran armies arrived, Elisha sent word by his servant to tell him to go wash seven times in the Jordan River. Angry that he was not greeted as a great commander, he was not prepared to be told anything. He had brought 750 pounds of silver, 150 pounds of gold, and ten beautifully made sets of clothing. The prophet of God, Elisha, was not impressed.

The commander turned on his heels and stomped away like a bratty child, angry that he had not been greeted by Elisha, that he hadn't been given an audience with the great prophet, that the material things he'd brought were not appreciated, and that he had been told, like a slave, to wash seven times in the nasty, dirty waters of Jordan, especially knowing there were clean rivers in the near area.

As he began to prepare to leave, his officers called out to him and tried to reason with him. They suggested, "What would it hurt to at least try?" They reasoned if he had been told to do something difficult, he would have done it. So why not something simple?

Their reasoning caused him to go. Seven times he dipped up and down in the muddy river, and behold, he was cured! His heart stopped for a moment as the realization became clear. Not one spot was anywhere on his body! His officers were stunned and started yelling with joy, shouting praises of thanksgiving to Elisha.

Coming out of the water and into his chariot, he swiftly drove his horses to Elisha's home. Knocking at the door, he offered everything to him: the silver, the gold, and the clothing. Elisha would not take any. To Elisha, that would be paying for a healing from Jehovah, and God could not be bought.

Now Naaman bowed low and said, "I know there is no other God like Jehovah. Him alone I will worship." Then taking the dirt from the ground of Israel, he swore, "Even when I have to take the king to pray, I will place this dirt under my knees so Jehovah knows I am worshiping only Him."

As he left Elisha, the servant waited and hid until he was almost out of sight. Then he stopped him on the road and asked Naaman to give him what he asked for. "Of course," Naaman said, and he gave him more than he requested. The servant then hid his treasures in the house. Upon the servant's return to Elisha, the prophet asked where he had been.

He said, "Nowhere."

Elisha said, "You are lying."

The servant turned white as snow from leprosy.

Time had passed for the child, and every day the commander was gone, she prayed. She told Jehovah she would trust in Him that the master of this house would be prayed over by Elisha and be healed. Sounds of chariots and horses approaching could be heard in the distance. Her mistress ran to the windows of her room, looking to see if he was returning.

With joy, she exclaimed, "He's coming! He's on the road!"

The child looked too and was excited. She was confident that Jehovah had heard her prayer and her master would no longer have leprosy.

When he got to the door, they could hear him shouting with great joy. He ran up the steps of the second and third floor, threw open the doors, and picked up the mistress, twirling her around as if to dance. Around and around they danced, laughing with delight. He was healed, he told her, completely healed of leprosy.

As he pulled up his sleeves and opened his shirt for her to see, she kissed him and then his chest and his neck. Both were so happy. The child went into her room to give them privacy.

The morning sun rose as if it knew a joyful celebration was happening behind the castle doors. The child rose, bathed, brushed her hair, and put on a new servant dress she had been saving for this celebration. She tied her hair to one side with a lovely hair barrette that her mistress had given her.

Going into the kitchen to pick up the breakfast tray, she stopped and picked some fresh flowers, and she placed them in a small vase to sit on the tray. She smiled and could hardly keep from singing. She was so happy.

Fear was gone, and in its place was that feeling of wishing she was home and could tell her mother and poppa what had happened. They understood about Jehovah and the prophet Elisha. Even in uncertain times, they had told her that Jehovah watches over us. She was no longer fearful in this place, but she knew when she got older, she would find a way to return to Samaria in northeastern Israel to reunite with her family.

As she entered the room, she saw her master was sitting in a chair by her mistress's bed. She quietly served her tray to her mistress. She looked across at him and saw his eyes light up when he viewed the flowers. He smiled at his wife and then requested for her to stay. She waited.

Now he stood, tall and regal in his uniform, a look she found somewhat disarming, but she had grown to like him some. He gazed at her, and she stayed very still, eyes downcast.

He spoke. "Tomorrow you are leaving. Please prepare your items and what you want to take. I will be taking you back to your homeland."

She was stunned. Surely she had not heard correctly! Puzzled, she lifted her eyes to see if he was making a joke of her, but no, he was smiling. So was her mistress.

This day would be forever in her mind. The horse and the chariot carried a ten-year-old across the border into Israel, over the watery river edges. The world, it seemed, had turned greener than she could ever remember and more beautiful. She would never forget.

As they neared the river where she had played that day, tears filled her eyes. The commander, her master, stepped out of his chariot and lifted her from his officer's horse. His eyes glistened as if they were full of tears. She watched as he kneeled down on one knee, which made him more her height. Taking her tiny hands in his big hand, he raised them to his lips and kissed them.

Forgiveness is a powerful tool. The commander asked her to please forgive him for taking her away. She was speechless. Her red tresses of hair, now windblown, bobbed up and down as she quietly said that he was forgiven.

Jehovah had performed more than one miracle through the prophet Elisha. Jehovah had changed an enemy into a friend. He had given hope where there seemed to be none for this child. Jehovah had given purpose for the ugliness and cruelty by turning it into good for His namesake. As the commander rose to get on his chariot, he took a bag from the front area and gave it to her. Waving goodbye, he turned and rode away in the direction he had come.

Homecomings are whatever you want to make them. This child was so happy to be home, and with the thrill of going home racing through every part of her body, her legs began to run. She wasn't that far, but it seemed far because she had been gone so long. She knocked on her family's door, and there they stood. She saw her poppa, along with the shock on his face and the joy in his eyes as he lifted her up. He hugged her as he yelled for her mother.

Her beautiful mother, seeing her, fell on the floor at their feet. She was overcome with tears, and her brother grabbed her and tried to take her from her poppa. This day would be etched in her mind until she died.

This child handed the heavy bag to her poppa. Inside were 150 pieces of gold.

Shocked again, the poppa asked, "Where? Where?"

"From the commander as he left. He gave it to me for our family."

Jehovah reigned in this family as they celebrated with neighbors and friends. Jehovah has done great things.

 CHALK TALK

Joyful and Happy
Proverbs 17:22; Psalm 118:24; Psalm 119:11; 1 Peter 2:1–25; Matthew 15:18

Listen to Your Parents
Ephesians 6:1–3; Exodus 20:12; Proverbs 1:8–9; Proverbs 22:15; Psalm 103:13

Fear and Anxiety
Philippians 4:6–7; Hebrews 13:6; Deuteronomy 31:6; John 14:27; 1 Peter 5:7; Psalm 27:7

Being Quiet
Proverbs 17:24; Ecclesiastes 3:7; James 1:19; 1 Peter 3:15; Hebrew 12:14a; Psalm 141:3; Psalm 27:14

Obedience to Those over You
Hebrews 13:17; Romans 13:1; Titus 2:9; Ephesians 6:5; 1 Timothy 6:1; Colossians 3:22; Romans 13:2

Purpose of God
Psalm 57:2; Jeremiah 29:11; Jeremiah 32:19; Proverbs 19:21; Psalm 33:11

Faith of a Child
Matthew 18:3; Luke 18:7; Proverbs 22:6; Psalm 8:2; Psalm 127:3; Matthew 18:4; Isaiah 54:13

Intercede in Prayer
Matthew 21:22; Ephesians 6:10–18; John 16:23–24; Matthew 7:11; Hebrews 7:25; John 14:6; James 5:16

Rewarded
1 Corinthians 15:58; Galatians 6:9; Proverbs 3:3–4; Proverbs 18:16; James 1:12; Deuteronomy 5:33; Proverbs 11:18; 1 Peter 5:6, 245–246

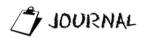 JOURNAL

Being frightened and enslaved, how would you turn a wrong into a possibility of freedom? Write about the ways of being obedient, calm, and attentive to the situation. Use your imagination. Then write how a place of no escape might be an opportunity to change the area you are living in or where you feel trapped. The scriptures give you a lead for new thinking. Do you agree?

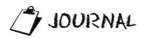 JOURNAL

THE DREAMER

MARK 5:35-43

Fragrance drifts across her face. These are the flowers she knows. The child is familiar with the scents of carnations, lilies, and gladiolas as she floats into the garden. She is twelve, and her mother has taught her about caring for these beautiful flowers. As an only child, she is guarded carefully. She has a quiet personality. Very content and happy, she loves learning. She is trying to move as this feeling of illness overtakes her. She lies still, hoping it will pass. Her skin is hot, like the sun is touching it. Drops of dampness cover her face. She tries to call her mother, but no sound is heard.

She continues to float. Her eyes fall upon the roses, and the smell overwhelms her. She allows the roses and spicy viburnums to fill her senses. Eyes now open, she lies quietly so as not to disturb the movement of each flower as it releases its presence into her soul. Oh, her laughter erupts as she now looks. Her eyes gaze upon the flowers' beauty. Her greatest joy is trimming with her mother, gathering bunches of flowers for the table. She is content.

Shortly, or so it seems, she is floating like the clouds beside her and gliding among the galaxy of stars and rays of sunlight shooting across the air. She continues floating, yet the fragrance is so near, and calmness is real. She does not move. Her mind is still, but her senses are aware. Floating causes her to relax completely, as she now sees glorious colors like a rainbow, sparkling as the rays of light touch them ever so gently.

She recognizes the gems, as she has seen them in jewels. Here, it's as if great slabs are made from jasper, blue lapis, and greens of different shades. And oh, the reds are stunning as well as the softer sky blue and shades of pinks with orange. Her eyes take in so much. She's not sure if she can contain it all.

Her ears catch a sound. It comes closer. First it is like a humming. As she floats, it appears to sound like more than a few voices. It's a host of voices saying, "Glory to God in the highest heaven" (Luke 2:14 NIV). She wants to sing too, but for some reason she does not. But in awe, she listens to the words over and over as the notes change to make the most beautiful sounds she has ever heard.

As she floats, she is now passing by a table. She gazes upon it, and her sense of taste comes alive. Elegance looms as a table beyond her vision is set with golden goblets; golden, glistening plates; and glowing, sparkling silver. As she views this massive forever table, her taste buds come alive in her mouth. She can almost taste the desired deep-purple grapes, the rosy pomegranates, the rich and appetizing figs surrounded by bright-yellow lemons, and deep-green kiwi fruits, a true favorite she loves.

Crystals are everywhere, sprinkled around the plates and goblets. She is sure they are diamonds. Elegance has no price tag. It just is. Deep-green foliage-filled basins stretch down this massive, grand table. It helps to hold the abundant flowers. They fill the air with the fragrance she had smelled before. The most prominent is the rose.

Taste buds are fighting to taste the foods when suddenly she feels a touch. She looks but sees nothing. Again, the touch is tender, and even though she is floating in the clouds, it causes her to look once again. But the cloud next to her causes a moment of not seeing. Sounds of laughter reach her ears. Her taste buds are more alive as she smells the foods.

Hearing someone quietly speaking in her dream, she opens her eyes and focuses immediately. She feels Him take her hand, and then He speaks, *"Talitha koum!"* (This means "Little girl, I say to you, get up!" [Mark 5:41 NIV].) She stands up and begins to walk around. He tells the onlookers to give her something to eat. Her poppa asks if she knows this is Jesus.

"Yes," she states. He is the fragrance she smelled, the song she heard, the hand she touched, the fruit of the vine that she had longed to taste. Her eyes recognize the Master.

Looking at this man named Jesus reassures her. She wants to eat, but she wants Him to stay. He does. The people, whom the mother had called, are mourning. That is, they were called when someone had passed away. Now they stand, looking with amazement. She takes His hand and leads Him to their table.

Her poppa is beaming with joy. Her mother has a tear-stained face filled with gladness and relief. The servants are so funny. They set the table, but they keep staring at this man named Jesus. At the table, He speaks about the kingdom to come and the streets made of transparent gold, trees and flowers, and walls of jasper. As he speaks, she realizes that while she was "sleeping," she had dreamed of the place He is talking about.

When Jesus leaves to return to Galilee, the family is overjoyed with thankful hearts. They bid Him farewell, knowing they will see Him again one day.

Her poppa had heard how Jesus was a great healer, and when he saw how sick his daughter was, he had traveled to bring Him to heal his only child, his beloved daughter. Since Jesus came, her sickness is gone, her fever has been destroyed, and she is perfectly well, like a joyful twelve-year-old should be. Her neighbors all talked throughout the village about this man named Jesus.

At night, we go to the family of Jairus. He, a ruler at the synagogue in Capernaum, sits, speaking with his wife and daughter. He believes this Jesus is the Messiah. He states, "Jesus has no reason to be selfish. He has no home or dwelling. Yet by the words from His mouth and the touch of His hand, he is healing many multitudes, as He did our daughter. Let us accept Him as the Messiah we have longed for in the land of Israel. Our hearts want to share all He has done for us. We will be a witness to His power and His goodness."

From that day forward, Jairus's family spreads the good news all over Capernaum. This little girl's poppa leaves the synagogue so he can teach the people about Jesus.

Often this child, when going to sleep, finds great peace reliving the dream she had and feeling the peace that filled every fiber of her mind, heart, and soul. Her sleep is peaceful. She vows to herself to never forget.

CHALK TALK AND JOURNAL

After you have read *The Dreamer*, journal your thoughts on how you think heaven might be and what would attract you the most to make sure you go.

Joann Jordan

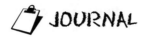 JOURNAL

SALVATION IS A GIFT

God so loved the world He gave His only son, that whoever believed in Him would not perish but have eternal life" (John 3:16 NIV).

This is a gift from God. Because of Jesus Christ's death on the cross and then His resurrection from the dead three days later, we know that death cannot hold us. Then Jesus Christ ascended back to the Father. Now, because Jesus paid the price for our sins at Calvary, we too can have eternal life when we pass from this life into the next, if we ask for forgiveness of our sins and accept Him into our hearts.

Printed in the United States
By Bookmasters